GREAT DISASTERS

THE CHERNOBYL CATASTROPHE

GRAHAM RICKARD

Illustrated by PETER BULL

The Bookwright Press
New York · 1989

Great Disasters

The Chernobyl Catastrophe
The Hindenburg Tragedy
The Eruption of Krakatoa
The Fire of London

The Destruction of Pompeii
The San Francisco Earthquake
The Space Shuttle Disaster
The Sinking of the Titanic

First published in the
United States in 1989 by
The Bookwright Press
387 Park Avenue South
New York, NY 10016

First published in 1988 by
Wayland (Publishers) Limited
61 Western Road, Hove
East Sussex BN3 1JD

© Copyright 1988
Wayland (Publishers) Ltd

Library of Congress Cataloging-in-Publication Data

Rickard, Graham.
    The Chernobyl catastrophe/Graham Rickard.
        p.   cm. — (Great disasters)
    Bibliography: p.
    Summary: Describes the events and aftermath of
the 1986 nuclear reactor explosion in Chernobyl and
discusses its long term effects and the future
implications for nuclear power plants.
    ISBN 0-531-18236-3
    1. Chernobyl Nuclear Accident, Chernobyl,
Ukraine, 1986 — Juvenile literature.
[1. Chernobyl Nuclear Accident, Chernobyl,
Ukraine, 1986. 2. Nuclear power plants —
Accidents.]   I. Title.   II. Series.
TK1362.S65R53 1989   88-5956
363.1'79 – dc19   CIP
                                                    AC

Consultant: David J. Dancy,
    Senior Information Officer,
    United Kingdom Atomic Energy Authority

Front cover: *A helicopter circles Chernobyl's stricken Reactor 4 a few days after the explosion.* Inset: *Fire officers attempt to wash radioactive dirt off houses in Kiev shortly after the disaster.*

Words that are printed **bold** the first time they appear in the text are explained in the glossary.

Phototypeset by Oliver Dawkins Ltd,
Burgess Hill, West Sussex
Printed in Italy by G. Canale & C.S.p.A., Turin

CONTENTS

RADIATION ALERT

On the morning of Monday, April 28, 1986 a **radiation** detector at the Forsmark nuclear power station in Sweden triggered an alarm. The detector was showing a radiation count of 100 **micro-rems** an hour, compared with the usual rate of 4 micro-rems. The managers of the power station were convinced that they had a massive leak of **radioactivity** and started to make frantic checks of every part of the plant. A hundred workers stayed at the plant to control the emergency, while the remaining 800 were quickly taken to a safe place. Local residents were warned of the

dangers on the radio, while teachers gave **iodine** tablets to hundreds of local schoolchildren to reduce the effects of radiation poisoning. Emergency rescue teams went into action, as the Swedish police completely sealed off the power station. High levels of radiation were reported elsewhere in Sweden and Finland, where the level was now six times higher than normal.

When Denmark and Norway also reported a sudden, massive increase in radioactivity, scientists began to look elsewhere for the cause of the leak. Basing their calculations on the speed and direction of the wind, Swedish experts pinpointed the leak at the **nuclear** power station at Chernobyl in the **USSR**, over 1,500km (900mi) away. They also estimated that the radiation levels were similar to those that would have been released by a fairly small **nuclear bomb** exploding at the site of the power station. Their suspicions were soon backed up by American spy **satellites**, which detected intense heat at Chernobyl. It became obvious that there had been a huge explosion and fire at the plant, releasing a large amount of radioactive material into the **atmosphere**.

Above *Satellite photographs such as this helped to pinpoint Chernobyl's reactor* (**circled**) *as the source of radiation.*

International reaction

The Swedish authorities were extremely angry with the **Soviet** government, which had not issued any warning.

Above *Radiation checks at the Forsmark nuclear power station on April 28, 1986.*

As Soviet officials had maintained their silence for two days, politicians from many countries criticized them for their stubborn secrecy and pointless denials that the accident had happened.

In the United States, President Reagan declared:

"The Soviets owe the world an explanation. A full account of what happened at Chernobyl and what is happening now, is the least the world community has a right to expect."

Above *A train in Denmark is discovered to be contaminated with radiation.*

In the absence of any solid information from the USSR, wild rumors began to circulate, telling of thousands of deaths, and whole cities living in terror. More realistically, some American experts predicted that there would be a **meltdown** of the **core** of the **reactor**, which would cause even worse **contamination**.

Inside the USSR, people were not told of the accident, nor were they warned of the dangers from the radiation it had caused. Even the immediate area around the power station was not **evacuated** until thirty-six hours after the accident. As an enormous cloud of deadly radioactivity swept over the countryside, most Soviets went about their daily business unaware of the contamination in the air and water, and in the food they were eating. It was eighteen days before the Soviet leader, Mikhail Gorbachev, finally appeared on television to inform the nation about the accident and its effects.

NUCLEAR NIGHTMARE

For decades, many people have been worried by the possible dangers of nuclear power, and the Chernobyl disaster confirmed their worst fears. As the USSR slowly released information, it became obvious that the explosion at Chernobyl was the world's worst nuclear accident.

The catastrophe started on Friday, April 25, 1986. Engineers at the plant carried out an experiment in an **unauthorized** manner that went against all regulations.

It involved operating the plant at reduced power, with the **coolant** pumps slowed down. That started a **chain reaction** that led to the disaster.

Shortly after midnight, the coolant water began to boil inside the core. That caused a rapid rise in temperature in the core, and a sudden, uncontrollable surge of power from the reactor. Some of the safety systems and alarms had been switched off during the experiment.

Below *The nuclear chain reaction, known as nuclear fission. A neutron hits a uranium atom, causing it to split, releasing large amounts of energy and more neutrons.*

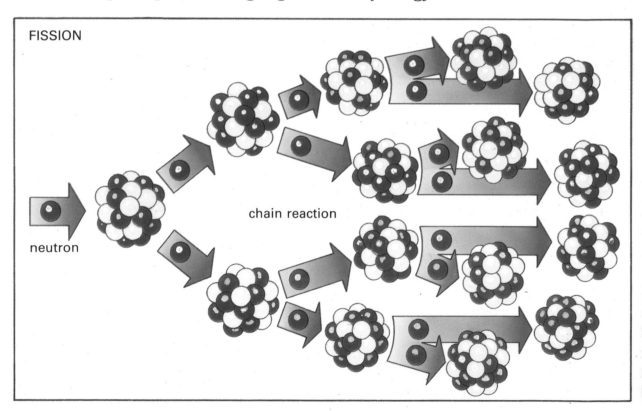

FISSION

chain reaction

neutron

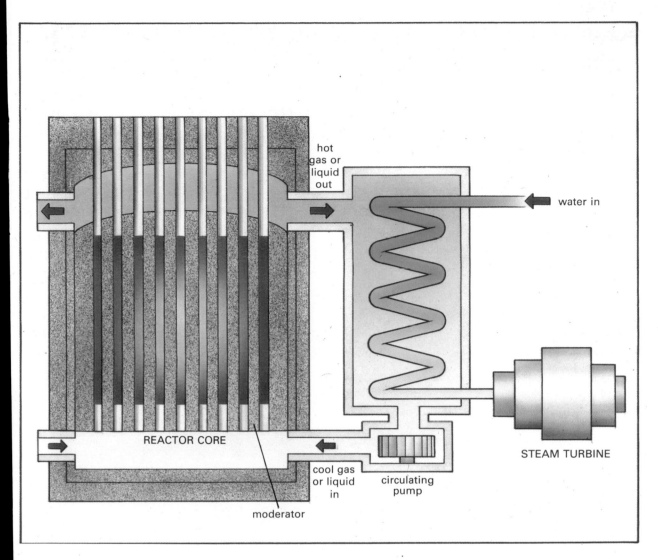

hot gas or liquid out

water in

REACTOR CORE

STEAM TURBINE

cool gas or liquid in

circulating pump

moderator

Above *A diagram showing a typical reactor. At Chernobyl the core became so hot that the moderator was set on fire.*

By the time the operator pressed the emergency shutdown button, it was too late – the reactor was already out of control. The massive power surge caused the fuel and water pipes in the core to overheat, melt and disintegrate. Fragments of fuel shot into the surrounding water, causing steam explosions that broke the core and blew off the **pile cap**. The explosions broke open the steel around the **graphite moderator**, which then caught fire. Meanwhile, **hydrogen** produced in the core exploded on contact with the air in the reactor hall. The explosion smashed the roof and walls of the building and shot radioactive material into the atmosphere.

Panic inside the reactor

Eyewitness accounts tell of general panic, but also of individual bravery. Twenty people were working in the power plant at the time of the accident. The explosion, which witnesses said "sounded like distant thunder," immediately alerted everyone in the area. Inside the power plant building no one was sure what had happened, and a series of frantic telephone calls made them none the wiser. One scientist finally ran down the maze of corridors and found the plant's newest reactor ablaze. A witness later said:

> "They had brought in firemen who were trying to put the fire out with water and chemicals. They were sure they could get it under control."

Later events proved that the fire officers were not prepared for such an accident.

Below *Workers run for their lives as explosions rip through the floor of the reactor hall.*

The enormous explosion started a fire inside the reactor, as the temperature of the core continued to rise. As red-hot and highly radioactive debris fell from the sky, scores of smaller fires were started all over the site. Local fire officers braved the **lethal** radiation in unsuccessful attempts to control the fires. In temperatures of up to 2,700°C (4,800°F), the fire officers' water turned to radioactive steam, merely adding to the contamination in the atmosphere. The first victim of the Chernobyl disaster was an operator named Valery Khodiemchuk, who was fatally scalded by escaping steam. His body has not been recovered and will remain buried in the reactor. Most of the other people killed soon after the explosion were fire officers, other emergency workers and the operators who remained at their posts in order to close down the other three reactors at the plant. Three hundred people, mainly fire officers, received very high radiation doses. The following day, 129 of them were flown to a special hospital in Moscow. Despite desperate efforts, twenty-nine people died.

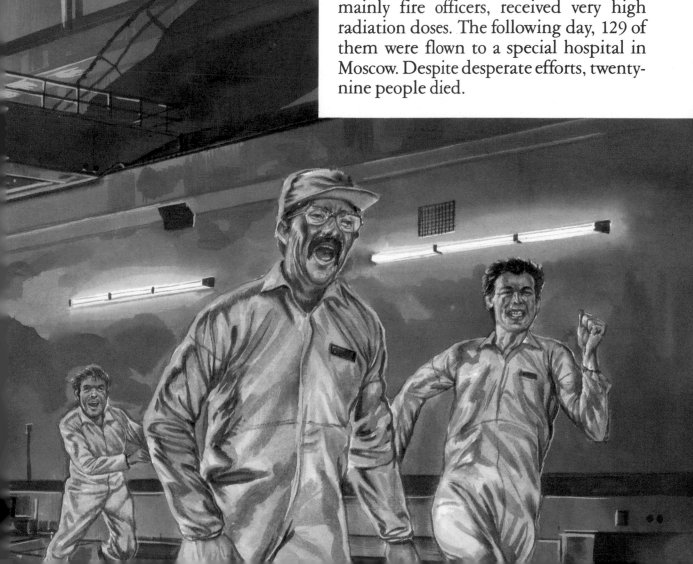

Fallout at Pripyat

At Pripyat, the town built to house the workers at the Chernobyl plant, residents were instructed to stay indoors overnight and iodine tablets were distributed. However, people were not given any advice or warnings. The next afternoon, as the fire still raged out of control, the whole town was evacuated in a convoy of 1,200 buses, stretching over 34km (20mi). Later, 135,000 people were evacuated from the entire area within 30km (19mi) of the plant. No one was allowed into the area, and soldiers in specially designed protective suits supervised the evacuation.

It was extremely fortunate that when the reactor went out of control, the wind blew the radiation away from Pripyat. Later, when everyone had been evacuated, the area was contaminated with twice the lethal level of radiation.

Hospitals in Kiev began to treat their first cases of **radiation sickness** and burns.

Below *Soviet television pictures show smoke escaping from the reactor.*

Yet Soviet officials still refused to explain what had happened. Rumors began to cause panic among the general public. A **radio ham** in Kiev, for example, incorrectly reported a death toll of 300, with thousands seriously ill.

By this time, radiation detectors had set off alarms all over Scandinavia, and governments around the world were demanding to know exactly what had happened at Chernobyl.

Above *This view from a helicopter shows the damage caused by the explosions.*

Right *A reactor of the type built at Chernobyl.*

10

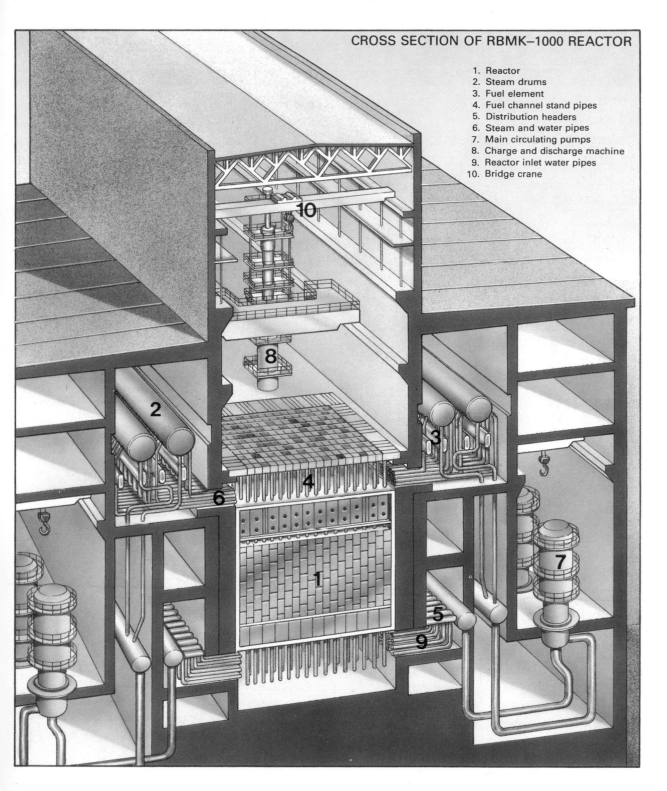

CROSS SECTION OF RBMK-1000 REACTOR

1. Reactor
2. Steam drums
3. Fuel element
4. Fuel channel stand pipes
5. Distribution headers
6. Steam and water pipes
7. Main circulating pumps
8. Charge and discharge machine
9. Reactor inlet water pipes
10. Bridge crane

FALLOUT OVER EUROPE

The explosion and fire at Chernobyl released about seven tons of highly radioactive material into the atmosphere, creating a poisonous cloud, which was later carried by the wind to almost every part of Europe and Scandinavia. The cloud consisted of particles of certain chemicals, called **radionuclides**. One of these, iodine 131, soon breaks down into harmless compounds, but others last much longer. For instance, caesium 137 lasts a very long time, is highly radioactive and is absorbed by plants, animals and humans. It causes radiation sickness, cancers and other serious illnesses.

Most of the people who lived around Chernobyl luckily escaped serious injury, because the accident happened at night.

Below *This map shows how the radioactive cloud gradually spread over Europe. It was later detected in the U.S.*

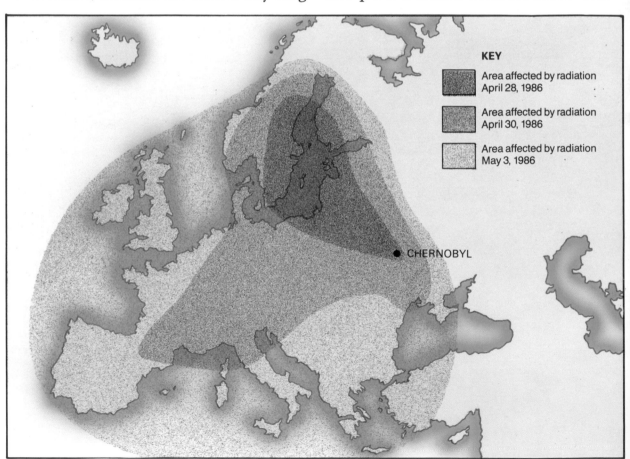

KEY

Area affected by radiation April 28, 1986

Area affected by radiation April 30, 1986

Area affected by radiation May 3, 1986

● CHERNOBYL

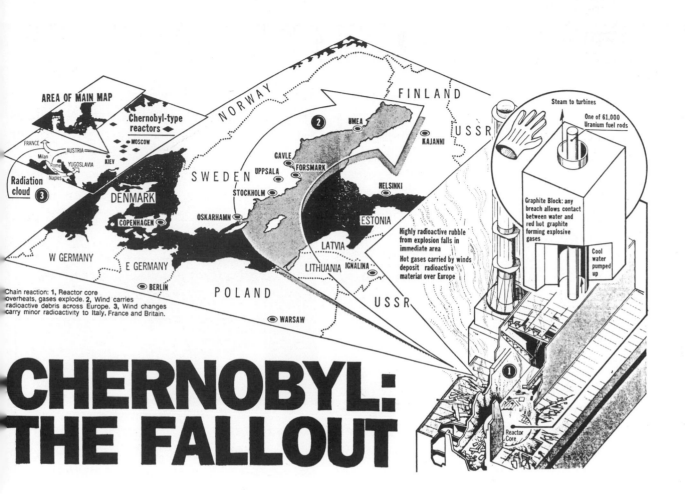

AREA OF MAIN MAP

Chernobyl-type reactors ◆

MOSCOW ◆

FRANCE ◆ AUSTRIA
Milan ◆ KIEV ◆
Rome ◆ YUGOSLAVIA
Naples

Radiation cloud **3**

NORWAY

FINLAND

USSR

2 UMEA

KAJANNI

GAVLE
FORSMARK
UPPSALA

HELSINKI

SWEDEN

STOCKHOLM

ESTONIA

OSKARHAMN

LATVIA

DENMARK

COPENHAGEN ◎

LITHUANIA IGNALINA ◎

W GERMANY

E GERMANY

◎ BERLIN

POLAND

USSR

◎ WARSAW

Chain reaction: 1, Reactor core overheats, gases explode. 2, Wind carries radioactive debris across Europe. 3, Wind changes carry minor radioactivity to Italy, France and Britain.

Highly radioactive rubble from explosion falls in immediate area

Hot gases carried by winds deposit radioactive material over Europe

Steam to turbines

One of 61,000 Uranium fuel rods

Graphite Block: any breach allows contact between water and red hot graphite forming explosive gases

Cool water pumped up

Reactor Core

1

CHERNOBYL: THE FALLOUT

Almost all of them were safely asleep indoors. It did not rain, so the **vaporized** material from the reactor stayed high above them in the atmosphere and was carried away by the wind. Some farm workers in Poland were not so fortunate, and were the first to suffer from the deadly **fallout**, as the rain washed the poisons onto their farms. Their skin itched, their eyes began to water, and then they started to vomit. Soon their hands swelled and their hair fell out as the radiation sickness gradually worsened.

Above *The British newspaper* The Sunday Times *ran this article on May 4, 1986. What it does not show is the fallout that was reaching Britain on that day!*

The radioactive cloud drifted across almost every European country. Thousands of migrating birds died after coming into contact with the air-borne poisons. Scandinavia in particular was badly affected, with heavy rainfall over Sweden leading to very high levels of radioactivity on the ground.

13

Above *The roads around Kiev are washed in an attempt to reduce the radiation.*

Emergency measures

At last, the first emergency measures were taken. In East Germany, where radiation levels were 100 times higher than normal, people were warned against eating fresh fish and fruit, and drinking milk and rainwater. Trucks and trains from Eastern Europe were hosed down by workers in gas masks and protective suits as they crossed the West German border, and the **EEC** imposed restrictions on the movement of food. Grass and crops were contaminated in West Germany, and cows were kept under cover in Holland.

The cloud first passed over Britain on May 2 and 3, and rain in parts of Scotland, Wales and the north of England on those days caused quite serious contamination. Radiation levels around the country were monitored and samples of food from

Above *Fruit grown in Eastern Europe is tested for signs of radioactivity before being sold. All kinds of crops grown in affected areas had to be tested.*

different areas were sent to London for testing. The British government issued warnings about the dangers of drinking fresh rainwater. It also banned sheep that had been grazing on contaminated grass from being slaughtered for food or moved to non-contaminated areas.

As radiation levels rose, governments in many countries imposed similar restrictions on the movement of animals and the sale of milk, which was found to contain worrying amounts of iodine 131.

In cows such poisons are concentrated very quickly, so milk can soon become the most deadly source of contamination, because much of it is drunk by babies and young children.

Meanwhile, at Chernobyl...

While every other country in Europe issued warnings to their people about the emergency and its dangers, those in the USSR remained uninformed. As Reactor 4 at Chernobyl continued to blaze and spew out its radioactive poisons, the Soviet authorities tried to smother the fire by dropping enormous amounts of sand, clay, lead and **boron** from helicopters. The radiation levels were so high that each helicopter pilot was allowed to fly only twenty-two missions, and in all 5,000 tons of material were dropped onto the plant. To prevent the core from burning its way down into the earth and contaminating water supplies, 400 engineers later tunneled beneath the reactor. They then poured in concrete to make a thick, heat-proof platform underneath the core.

Below *A helicopter drops sand and clay onto the burning reactor.*

PANIC IN KIEV

Kiev, the capital of the Ukraine, is 100km (62mi) south of Chernobyl. The citizens of Kiev thought it strange when all their buses disappeared from the city's streets. In fact, they were being used to evacuate people living near Chernobyl, but people in Kiev were told nothing.

Rumors spread

Patients started arriving at Kiev's Oktober hospital suffering from severe burns and radiation sickness.

Below *Kiev, with a population of 2.4 million, lies close to Chernobyl.*

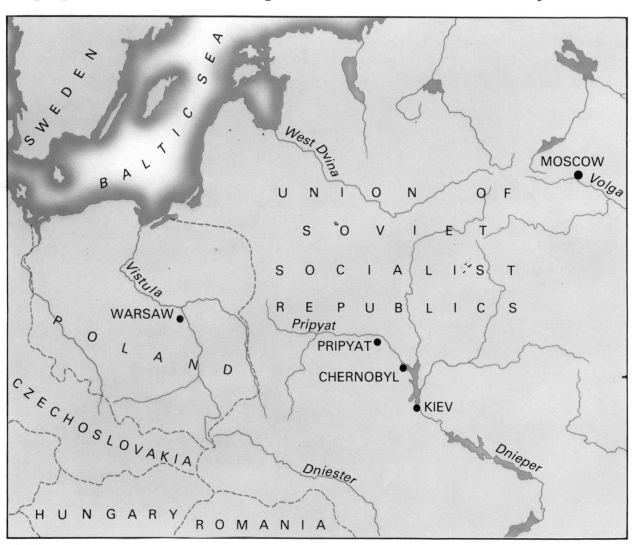

Above *Evacuees from Chernobyl are checked for radiation at a state farm.*

Right *Oleg and Mischa show a picture of their father, a fireman who was sent to Moscow for radiation treatment.*

Soon, rumors caused people to begin to panic. As foreigners were flown out from Kiev airport, they were watched by crowds of local people chanting, "We want to live too." Throughout the Ukraine, sales of vodka soared, after a rumor spread saying that alcohol gave protection against radiation sickness. Since the authorities maintained their official silence about Chernobyl, Kiev residents were not warned against eating contaminated food or drinking radioactive milk or rainwater.

A city without children
Soviet officials finally began to realize the seriousness of the situation, and they issued warnings on local radio and television stations. Kiev suddenly became a city without children, as a quarter of a million schoolchildren under the age of ten were evacuated to safer areas. As the radioactive cloud passed directly over the city, residents were instructed to stay indoors with their windows shut; to bathe daily; and to scrub their homes to remove contamination. People pulled their children in from the streets, and kept their doors and windows shut tight. Streets and buildings were constantly hosed down and all trains and roads to stations and airports were packed, as thousands rushed to leave the city.

Above *Workers wearing protective clothing prepare to enter the reactor.*

Above *Engineers begin the work of covering Reactor 4 with a concrete shell.*

Containing Chernobyl

At Chernobyl, engineers were finally bringing the damaged reactor under control. Emergency teams took turns entering the most dangerous areas, using stop watches to time how long they were exposed to high-level radiation. **Remote-controlled** vehicles and protected manned vehicles were used to clear away debris from around the plant. Walls and ditches had to be built to keep water from draining out of the plant into the Pripyat and Dnieper rivers, which supply most of Kiev's water. Vast areas of contaminated **topsoil** were removed, and the roofs of houses in Pripyat were hosed down to remove radioactive matter.

Pripyat is likely to remain a ghost town for a long time. Towns have been built to house some of the 135,000 people who were evacuated, and the area around Chernobyl, now overgrown and deserted has been enclosed by a 200km (124mi) fence.

The final stage of the cleaning-up operation was the construction of an enormous concrete box, twenty floors high, to enclose the entire reactor. This was built with **ventilation shafts**, containing sensors to monitor the state of the nuclear core of the reactor.

At last, Soviet leaders began to release information about the disaster, and gratefully accepted offers of help from foreign governments and experts. Protective suits from Britain, and remote-controlled vehicles from Italy and West Germany were used to clean up the site. Also, some American surgeons flew to Moscow and Kiev to treat those people who were most seriously affected by the radiation. Unfortunately for some of them, there was little that even the most advanced medicine could do. As the death toll rose, one American doctor predicted that over 100,000 Soviets would need special medical check-ups for the rest of their lives. This will be necessary in order to watch for signs of cancer and other illnesses caused by exposure to radiation.

Below *In addition to the shell, a concrete layer was inserted beneath the reactor to protect the local water supply.*

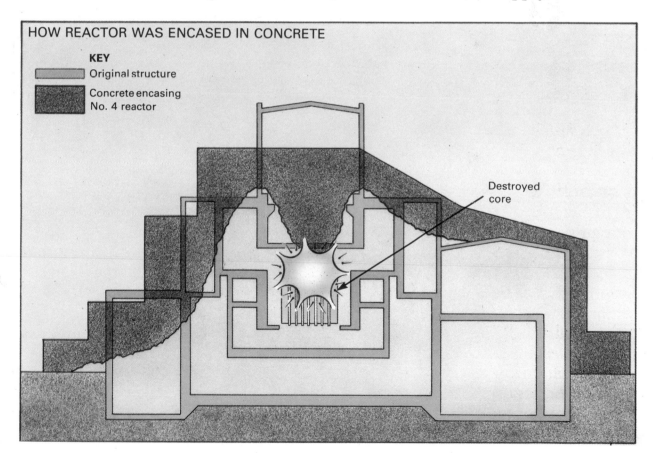

HOW REACTOR WAS ENCASED IN CONCRETE

KEY
Original structure
Concrete encasing No. 4 reactor

Destroyed core

WHO WAS TO BLAME?

The Soviet authorities started an official inquiry into the Chernobyl accident soon after it happened. The inquiry aimed to establish whether the disaster was a freak accident or whether something similar might happen at Soviet or other nuclear power stations. The USSR relies on nuclear power to generate 10 to 15 percent of its electricity; this will have to be generated in some other way if nuclear power is deemed to be unsafe.

Below *The reactor hall at Chernobyl seen before the explosion.*

A Soviet design

The plant at Chernobyl, which first opened in 1977, had four reactors, each producing 1,000 **megawatts** (MW) of electricity, with two more being built nearby. These are known as RBMK reactors and are built to a design that is unique to the USSR. Like all nuclear reactors, they work like giant kettles, using the heat from splitting **atoms** of **uranium dioxide** fuel to produce steam, which drives **turbines** to produce electricity. Rods of boron control the reactor by absorbing some of the **neutrons** that cause **fission**.

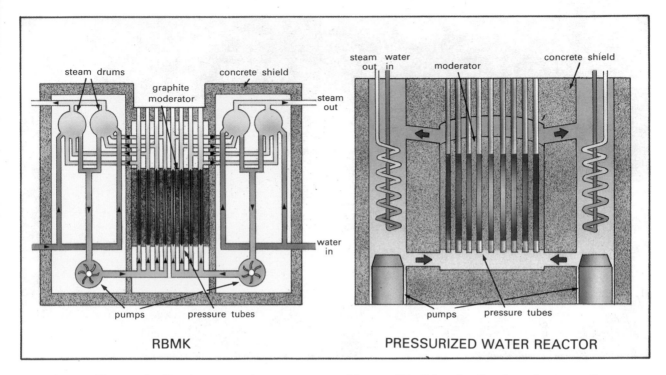

steam drums
graphite moderator
concrete shield
steam out
water in
pumps
pressure tubes
RBMK

steam out
water in
moderator
concrete shield
pumps
pressure tubes
PRESSURIZED WATER REACTOR

When Chernobyl's Reactor 4 was put into production in 1985, the chief engineer Vyacheslav Akinfeyev proudly wrote in the Communist Party's journal *Kommunist*:

"Chernobyl is much cleaner than a thermal (coal or oil-fired) station of identical capacity. It does not eject harmful fuel combustion products into the air, and does not consume oxygen for the burning of fuel."

Pripyat, a modern city of 45,000 people was built to house the people working at Chernobyl. It had flower-lined streets and apartment blocks set among trees. The average age of Pripyat's residents was very young – only twenty-six – and the mayor, Vladimir Voloshko, was proud of his town. He declared, "We believe that

Above *Unlike the Soviet-designed RBMK, the pressurized water reactor has a thick concrete shield to limit damage caused by an accident.*

Pripyat should be as clean as the power plant," and he told journalists that, "Working in any nuclear power station is safer than driving your car."

Just two months before the catastrophe, the magazine *Soviet Life* praised Chernobyl for its safety standards and said:

"Even if the incredible should happen, the automatic control and safety systems would shut down the reactor in a matter of minutes."

The article also quoted the Minister of Power as saying, "The chances of a meltdown are one in 10,000 years."

Bad design?

Journalists who visited Chernobyl told a different story: they reported that neither they nor the workers had been given radiation detector badges (to warn them of the presence of high levels of radiation), hard hats or coveralls. In addition, a month before the accident, the newspaper *Literaturna Ukraina* reported on its front page that the Chernobyl plant was being built too fast, with defective materials, and that serious mistakes had already been built into the reactor.

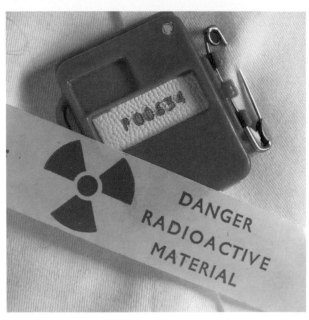

Above *A radiation detector badge worn by workers in nuclear power stations.*

Above *A Western nuclear worker with his protective suit.*

Many Western experts feel that it was the design of the reactor that was at fault. As early as 1946, the design was flatly rejected in Britain as being too dangerous. British engineers visited the USSR in 1976, examined the RBMK reactors and later expressed serious doubts about the design. In the West, all water-cooled reactors are enclosed in a huge concrete "containment vessel" – a thick shell that traps any radioactivity in the event of the core getting out of control. The Chernobyl reactor had no such protection, and the reactor hall was not strong enough to withstand an explosion. There was only a limited emergency cooling system. The reactor was safe only as long as the operator did not make a mistake.

Another weakness lay in the thin **zirconium** pipes that carried boiling water through the core of graphite and nuclear fuel. In the event of a fire, zirconium melts at 1,000°C (1,832°F), giving off an explosive mixture of hydrogen and oxygen, and creates, in effect, a powerful bomb.

Human error

The official inquiry blamed human errors by Chernobyl's operators as the main cause

Below *A new reactor under construction. The disaster at Chernobyl has caused experts to reconsider reactor design.*

of the accident, but it also pointed out basic faults in the reactor design. At the time of the accident, the USSR had fourteen large RBMK reactors in operation, with one about to enter service, and seven more under construction. They were all closed down until the inquiry had finished its investigations, and certain alterations were made to the reactors before they went back into service. Operators have been trained in new emergency procedures, and new safety measures have been introduced. Yet many experts are still concerned about the safety of RBMK reactors.

LONG-TERM EFFECTS

By mid-1988, thirty-one people had died, and hundreds more were seriously ill as a direct result of the world's worst nuclear accident. Over 80,000 Russian people still cannot return to their homes, and an area about the size of the state of Oregon, in the heart of the Ukraine's farming region, will be an uninhabitable wasteland for decades. Particles of Chernobyl's vaporized core can still be detected high in the **troposphere**, posing a deadly threat for future generations wherever it falls. Traces of fallout from the plant have already been detected as far away as the United States and the Philippines.

The unseen threat

Radiation from radioactive particles damages the cells that make up our bodies. It does this in a way that can cause leukemia and other cancers, and even genetic defects in future generations. Recent research shows that there may not be any such thing as a "safe minimum dose" of radiation. Some scientists estimate that between 50,000 and 100,000 people in Europe will die from cancers due to Chernobyl in the next thirty years. Even very small levels of exposure, especially in children and old people, can weaken the natural resistance to diseases and infections. So, the widespread contamination caused by Chernobyl may damage the health of millions of people.

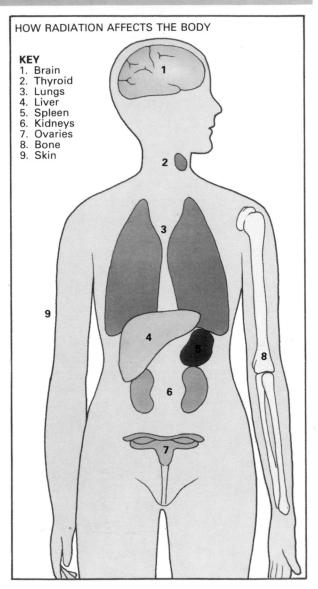

HOW RADIATION AFFECTS THE BODY

KEY
1. Brain
2. Thyroid
3. Lungs
4. Liver
5. Spleen
6. Kidneys
7. Ovaries
8. Bone
9. Skin

Above *Different types of radiation affect different parts of the body, sometimes causing cancer. For instance, iodine 131 affects the thyroid gland, while caesium 137 affects women's ovaries (see page 12).*

24

Farming has been badly affected by fallout in most European countries. In Lapland, over 40,000 reindeer were contaminated. They could not be used for food and had to be slaughtered. This was a disaster for the Lapp people, who depend on the wild reindeer herds for most of their needs.

Some foodstuffs have been found to be more affected than others: tomatoes, for example, don't seem to absorb much radioactivity, while berries do. Fish have been shown to concentrate the radioactivity, and cows quickly pass on the contamination from grass to their milk. The effects are lasting much longer than experts first expected, and in some areas radiation levels are actually rising.

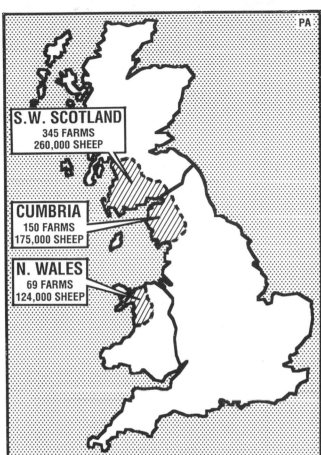

Above *This map shows the areas where the British government restricted the movement and slaughter of sheep.*

Caesium in the soil becomes concentrated in plants, and those plants are then eaten by animals. In Britain, the government expected the problem to last only a few weeks. But some scientists now fear that the movement and sale of sheep from contaminated areas may have to be restricted. This restriction may last for as long as thirty years in badly affected areas such as Cumbria in northern England.

Above *In Lapland thousands of reindeer had to be destroyed.*

Can reactors be safe?

The head of the Soviet fire service said that Chernobyl had proved that there was no such thing as a safe nuclear reactor, and that the disaster had cost the USSR billions of dollars in economic damage. It is impossible to calculate the total financial cost of the accident. Sweden alone suffered millions of dollars in damage to the farmers' crops and livestock. Throughout Europe, the tourist trade suffered as Americans and others canceled their European vacations because they feared contamination.

After the accident at Chernobyl, people throughout the world started to question the value and safety of using nuclear power to generate electricity. Within days of the accident, there were large anti-nuclear **demonstrations** in many European cities, and posters began to appear on walls in West Germany carrying the message "Chernobyl Is Everywhere."

Below *Nuclear power stations are spread right across Europe. It is easy to see from this map why the accident at Chernobyl must not be repeated.*

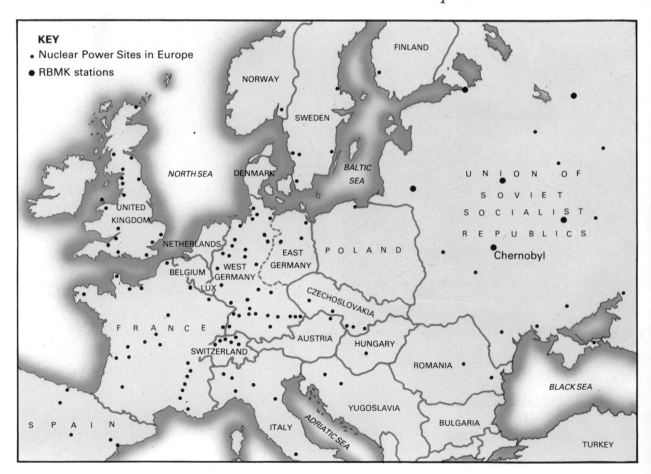

KEY
- Nuclear Power Sites in Europe
- RBMK stations

There have been
some cases of
areas becoming
contaminated by
nuclear waste,
despite careful
treatment such as
we see in these
photographs.

Above *Nuclear
waste is stacked in a
dry store.*

Right *Spent fuel
rods glow as they
cool off.*

Nuclear accidents

Before Chernobyl, there had been other, less serious nuclear accidents. In 1957, the British reactor at Windscale caught fire. Although some details of the accident were suppressed by the government to prevent public panic, it is known that a large amount of radioactive material was released into the atmosphere. In the following year, there was a large explosion, possibly involving nuclear waste, near the town of Kyshtym in the USSR.

The names of several villages in the area were later deleted from official Soviet maps. In 1979, the U.S. nuclear industry experienced its worst accident at the Three Mile Island plant in Pennyslvania, when a partial meltdown forced the evacuation of local residents.

Below *The Three Mile Island nuclear reactor. Radioactive material was leaked when the coolant failed in one of the two reactors.*

Above *Wind turbines generate electricity in California.*

Left *The sun's rays are used as a source of power in France.*

Alternative energy

With the Chernobyl accident following those at Windscale, Kyshtym and Three Mile Island, governments have started thinking seriously about alternative ways of producing electricity. Some favor going back to the use of coal and oil, others prefer harnessing the power of the sun, wind and waves. Sweden suffered badly from Chernobyl, and has already decided to close down all its nuclear plants by the year 2010. The United States stopped ordering new nuclear plants ten years ago, because of the safety risks and high costs. Australia, Denmark and New Zealand have all decided not to develop nuclear power.

Austria and the Philippines are dismantling their unused new nuclear plants. In Belgium, where nuclear power stations are often sited close to large towns and cities, many people now realize the dangers for the first time. Even in countries such as France, where nuclear power provides 70 percent of all electricity, the accident at Chernobyl has raised questions about the possible dangers.

Chernobyl showed that most countries are not prepared for such an emergency. The countries of the world must now decide whether the advantages of nuclear power justify the risk of another similar, or even worse, disaster.

GLOSSARY

Atmosphere The layer of gases, or air, that surrounds the earth.

Atom The smallest divisible part of an element, made up of protons, neutrons and electrons.

Boron A non-metallic element used in nuclear reactors. It absorbs neutrons and stops nuclear reactions.

Chain reaction A series of linked events that occur one after the other.

Contamination Pollution by chemicals, radioactivity, or other unwanted materials.

Coolant A liquid, such as water or oil, that circulates to cool engines or other kinds of machinery.

Core The part of a nuclear power reactor that contains the fuel.

Demonstration (Political demonstration) A group of people marching together to show their support for or against a political issue.

EEC The European Economic Community; a group of European countries that share economic policies.

Evacuate To leave (or to help others to leave) a dangerous place.

Fallout Radioactive contamination that falls from the atmosphere.

Fission The splitting of the nucleus of an atom.

Graphite A form of the chemical element carbon. It is often used as a moderator (see definition) in nuclear reactors.

Hydrogen A gas. When combined with oxygen it makes water.

Iodine A chemical element. Taking iodine tablets can help to reduce the possibility of radiation sickness by preventing the absorbtion of iodine 131.

Lethal Deadly, something that can kill.

Megawatt (MW) One million watts. A watt is a unit of electrical power.

Meltdown The point at which the core of a reactor becomes so hot that it melts down into the earth.

Micro-rem A unit of radioactivity, used in measuring effects on the body.

Moderator A material (such as graphite) that is used to speed up the nuclear chain reaction in the cores of nuclear reactors.

Neutron One of the tiny particles that makes up an atom.

Nuclear Involving the nucleus, or center, of an atom.

Nuclear bomb A bomb that gets its power from an uncontrolled nuclear chain reaction.

Pile cap The top cover of a reactor core (early reactors were called piles).

Radiation The sending and spreading out of energy, such as sunlight or nuclear particles.

Radiation sickness Illness caused by exposure to radioactivity.

Radioactivity The sending out of nuclear radiation.

Radio ham An amateur radio broadcaster.

Radionuclide A substance that sends out nuclear radiation.

Reactor A device in which a controlled nuclear reaction takes place.

Remote controlled Controlled from a distance, for example by radio signals.

Soviet Typical of, or relating to, the USSR.

Satellite A device that orbits the earth and uses special equipment to pick up information from one area and transmit the information over great distances to other areas.

Topsoil The upper layer of soil.

Troposphere The lowest layer of the atmosphere, about 16km (10mi) high.

Turbine A machine that spins at high speed to drive generators that produce electricity.

Uranium dioxide A chemical compound. It contains the radioactive metallic element uranium, which is used as a fuel for nuclear reactors.

Unauthorized Without permission.

USSR The Union of Soviet Socialist Republics.

Vaporize To turn a material into a gas.

Ventilation shaft A passage designed to allow air in and out of a room or building.

Zirconium A grayish-white metal, which is resistant to corrosion and radioactivity.

BOOKS TO READ

Bentley, Judith. *The Nuclear Freeze Movement.*
    Franklin Watts, 1984
Halacy, Don. *Nuclear Energy.* Franklin Watts, 1984
Hawkes, Nigel. *The Nuclear Arms Race.* Gloucester
    Press, 1986
Hawkes, Nigel. *Nuclear Safety.* Gloucester
    Press, 1987
Helgerson, Joel. *Nuclear Accidents.* Franklin Watts,
    1988.
Pringle, Laurence. *Arms Race or Human Race?*
    Morrow, 1987

Pringle, Laurence. *Nuclear Power: From Physics to
    Politics.* Macmillan, 1981
Taylor, L.B. Jr. *The Nuclear Arms Race.* Franklin
    Watts, 1982
Weiss, Ann E. *The Nuclear Arms Race – Can We
    Survive It?* Houghton Mifflin, 1983
Williams, Gene. B. *Nuclear War, Nuclear Winter.*
    Fanklin Watts, 1987

FURTHER INFORMATION

f you would like to find out more about the issues surrounding nuclear power, you can write to some
of the following:

Council for a Livable World
100 Maryland Avenue, NE
Washington, DC 20002

Karen Silkwood Fund
1324 N. Capitol Street
Washington, DC 20002

Mobilization for Survival
853 Broadway, Suite 418
New York, NY 10003

Physicians for Social Responsibility
1601 Connecticut Avenue, NW
Washington, DC 20009

SANE/FREEZE
711 G Street SE
Washington, DC 20003

Union of Concerned Scientists
26 Church Street
Cambridge, Mass. 02238

Worldwatch Institute
1776 Massachusetts Avenue, NW
Washington, DC 20036

INDEX

ACKNOWLEDGMENTS

The illustrations on pages 8-9 and 15 are by Peter Chasterton.

The publishers would like to thank the following for providing the photographs in this book: Associated Press *cover*; British Nuclear Fuels 22 (left), 25 (right); Camera Press 14 (left); Rex Features *cover* (inset), 5 (right), 10 (left and right), 14 (right), 18 (left and right); Topham Picture Library 4, 5 (left), 17 (left and right), 22 (right); United Kingdom Atomic Energy Authority 27 (left and right); Wayland Picture Library 23; Zefa Picture Library 25 (left), 28, 29 (left and right).